Armageddon
Bombs
and
Hail

Will Clark

Armageddon
Bombs
and
Hail

ISBN 13: 978-1720398868
ISBN 10: 1720398860

Published By
Motivation Basics
P.O. Box 6327
Diamondhead, MS 39525

Contents

It Begins

What was the beginning of that great battle, Armageddon? What caused it and how did it start? We've all heard this name many times, but what does it really mean? Basically, Armageddon is a battle between Good and Evil, and the two leaders of that great battle are Christ and Satan. But, how do we know this for certain? The Bible gives all the information and it's presented 'crystal clear,' as explained in Revelation, Chapter 4, verses 6 and 8:

"And before the throne there was a sea of glass like unto crystal: and in the midst of the throne, and round about the throne, were four beasts full of eyes before and behind. And the four beasts had each of them six wings about him; and they were full of eyes within: and they rest not day and night, saying, Holy, holy, holy, Lord God Almighty, which was, and is, and is to come." In summary, these beasts around the throne could see everything, everywhere, in the future and in the past crystal clear. And, what they saw, in the future, at the present, and in the past was written as the Book of Revelation. But, what did they see that would indicate this coming great battle? Chapters 10 and 12 give that 'crystal clear' answer.

Chapter 12 introduces the appearance of a great wonder in heaven, described in the first verse as 'a woman clothed with the sun, and the moon under her feet, and upon her head a crown of twelve stars.' This wonder represented Christianity. Then verse 3 began the explanation of the appearance of Satan:

"And there appeared another wonder in heaven; and behold a great red dragon, having seven heads and ten horns, and seven crowns upon his heads. 4) And his tail drew the third part of the stars of heaven, and did cast them to the earth: and the dragon stood before the woman (Christianity) which was ready to be delivered, for to devour her child (Christ) as soon as it was born." While those physical actions regarding the new religion were taking place on earth (those related to time, times, and half a time) a battle was also raging in Heaven. That's explained in verses beginning with verse 7:

"And there was a war in heaven: Michael and his angels fought against the dragon; and the dragon fought and his angels, 8) And prevailed not; neither was their place found any more in heaven. 9) And the great dragon was cast out, that old serpent, called the Devil, and Satan which deceiveth the whole world: he was cast out into the earth, and his angels were cast out with him." Then there was rejoicing in heaven and a warning to the inhabiters of the earth. Verse 10 continues:

"And I heard a loud voice saying in heaven, Now is come salvation and strength, and the kingdom of God, and the power of his Christ: for the accuser of our brethren is cast down, which accused them before our God day and night. 11) And they overcame him by the blood of the Lamb, and by the word of their testimony; and they loved not their lives unto the death. 12) Therefore rejoice, ye heavens, and ye that dwell in them. Woe to the inhabiters of the earth and of the sea! for the devil is come down unto you, having great wrath, because he knoweth that he hath but a short time." Then verse 17 reveals Satan's anger:

"And the dragon was wroth with the woman, and went to make war with the remnant of her seed, which keep the commandments of God and have the testimony of Jesus Christ." Chapter 10 then explains what happened when Satan came down to earth. This is from Apostle John's vision:

"And I saw another mighty angel come down from heaven, clothed with a cloud: and a rainbow upon his head, and his face was as it were the sun, and his feet as pillars of fire: 2) And he had in his hand a little book open: and he set his right foot upon the sea, and his left foot on the earth, 3) And cried with a loud voice, as when a lion roareth: and when he had cried, seven thunders uttered their voices. 4) And when the seven thunders had uttered their voices, I was about to write: and I heard a voice from heaven saying unto me, Seal up those things which the seven thunders uttered, and write them not."

These seven thunders were Satan and his six angels who had joined him when he was cast out of Heaven. These six were the 'third of the stars' mentioned in 12:4. The total of the stars was eighteen; the other twelve stars were those in the 'crown of twelve stars' in the first verse. This gave Satan the identity of the 'seventh' angel. Satan's threat against God continues in the next verse of Chapter 10:

"And the angel which I saw stand upon the sea and upon the earth lifted up his hand to heaven, 6) And sware by him that liveth for ever and ever, who created heaven, and the things that therein are, and the earth, and the things that therein are, and the sea, and the things which are therein, that there should be time no longer. 7) But in the days of the voice of the seventh angel, when he shall begin to sound, the mystery of God should be finished, as he hath declared to his servants the prophets."

Perhaps our current time is that time when Satan has begun to sound. He sounds through the voice of Babylon the Great which is the coded identity of Islam. Islam is, today, making great advances in her voice in society; as well as the respected place of religions. Islam is even considered by many, including the current Pope in Rome, as one of the three Abrahamic religions. Islam claims this status through their false suggestion that they are descended from Abraham's son Ishmael. Even

Muhammad himself refuted this claim. God gave a clue to this false claim through John's vision concerning that little book in Satan's hand. Verse 8 continues this vision:

"And the voice which I heard from heaven spake unto me again, and said, Go and take the little book which is open in the hand of the angel which standeth upon the sea and upon the earth. 9) And I went unto the angel, and said unto him, Give me the little book. And he (the voice from heaven) said unto me, Take it, and eat it up; and it shall make thy belly bitter, but it shall be in thy mouth sweet as honey. 10) And I took the little book out of the angel's hand, and ate it up; and it was in my mouth sweet as honey: and as soon as I had eaten it, my belly was bitter. 11) And he (the voice from heaven) said unto me, Thou must prophesy again, before many peoples, and nations, and tongues, and kings."

So, what happened to that little book into which John was told not to write? Clearly, God speaking from heaven told John not to include the words from those seven thunders into John's Words in the Book of Revelation. The words in that little book were bitter; against God. Who now has that little book; that book bitter enough to lead the war against God in heaven; and Christians? It's now that little book that guides Islam to be Satan's warriors against God that will conclude in that great Battle of Armageddon when Babylon the Great will be totally destroyed from the face of the earth. This conclusion is given in two places.

The first two verses in Chapter 18 proclaim, "And after these things I saw another angel come down from heaven, having great power and the earth was lightened with his glory. 2) And he cried mightily with a strong voice, saying, Babylon the great is fallen, is fallen, and is become the habitation of devils, and the hold of every foul spirit, and a cage of every unclean and hateful bird."

Words of victory over Babylon the great continue in verse 20:

"Rejoice over her, thou heaven, and ye holy apostles and prophets; for God hath avenged you on her. 21) And a mighty angel took up a stone like a great millstone, and cast it into the sea, saying, Thus with violence shall that great city Babylon be thrown down, and shall be found no more at all. 22) And the voice of the harpers, and musicians, and of pipers, and trumpeters, shall be heard no more at all in thee; and no craftsman, of whatsoever craft he be, shall be found anymore in thee; and the sound of a millstone shall be heard no more at all in thee; 23) And the light of a candle shall shine no more at all in thee; and the voice of the bridegroom and of the bride shall be heard no more at all in thee: for thy merchants were the great men of the earth; for by thy sorceries were all nations deceived. 24) And in her was found the blood of prophets, and of saints, and of all that were slain upon the earth."

Now let's return to that 'little book.' What was it and what was it used for? An article in Wikipedia helps give those answers. This is one of the informative links, titled, Muhammad's first revelation:

https://en.wikipedia.org/wiki/Muhammad%27s_first_revelation

"Muhammad's first revelation was an event described in Islam as taking place in 610 AD, during which the Islamic prophet, Muhammad was visited by the archangel Gabriel, who revealed to him the beginnings of what would later become the Quran. The event took place in a cave called Hira, located on the mountain Jabal an-Nour, near Mecca.

According to biographies of Muhammad, while on retreat in a mountain cave near Mecca (the cave of Hira), Gabriel appears before him and commands him to recite the first lines of chapter 96 of the

9

Quran. Muhammad's experience is mentioned in Surah 53:4–9:

"It is no less than inspiration sent down to him:
He was taught by one Mighty in Power,
Endued with Wisdom: for he appeared (in stately form);
While he was in the highest part of the horizon:
Then he approached and came closer,
And was at a distance of but two bow-lengths or (even) nearer;"[Qurar
53:4–9]

According to mainstream Islamic tradition, during one such occasior
while he was in contemplation, the archangel Gabriel appeared before
him in the year 610 AD and said, "Read", upon which he replied, "I am
unable to read". Thereupon the angel caught hold of him and embracec
him heavily. This happened two more times after which the ange
commanded Muhammad to recite the following verses:

"Proclaim! (or read!) in the name of your Lord who created: Createc
man from a clinging substance:

Recite, and your Lord is the most Generous,–
Who taught by the pen–
Taught man that which he knew not."[Quran 96:1–5]

Perplexed by this new experience, Muhammad made his way to home
where he was consoled by his wife Khadijah, who also took him to he
Ebionite cousin Waraqah ibn Nawfal. Waraqah was familiar witl
Jewish and Christian scriptures. Islamic tradition holds that Waraqah
upon hearing the description, testified to Muhammad's prophethood
and convinced Muhammad that the revelation was from God. Waraqal
said: "O my nephew! What did you see?" When Muhammad told hin
what had happened to him, Waraqah replied: "This is Namus (meanin;
Gabriel) that Allah sent to Moses. I wish I were younger. I wish I coulc

live up to the time when your people would turn you out." Muhammad asked: "Will they drive me out?" Waraqah answered in the affirmative and said: "Anyone who came with something similar to what you have brought was treated with hostility; and if I should be alive until that day, then I would support you strongly." A few days later Waraqah died." End of quote.

In conclusion, that angel who visited Muhammad in that cave with a book from which to read never said who he was. Someone later claimed it was God's representative, the angel Gabriel. Was the Koran given to Muhammad; or was the Koran created by those biographers who came after Muhammad? The information they present certainly suggests that Koran is the same little book the angel Satan held when he swore to remove God's time from Heaven. That little book, sweet in the mouth, but bitter in the belly, was Satan's written plan to war against God. Satan and his Islamic army will be defeated at the Battle of Armageddon, and Satan will finally be destroyed a thousand years later. This short message defines the reason John was commanded to write these things that became the Book of Revelation. Next, we begin the full story of preparations for the battle, and the battle itself.

Introduction

What was the purpose for the Book of Revelation? Was it to reveal the 'end of time' or was it to warn of a great disaster before that great end of time event? Perhaps this question has caused great confusion; and caused many to ignore that warning within. Three books in the Bible give some clarity to this question.

Matthew, Chapter 24, verses 35-36, gives an answer to that end of time question: "Heaven and earth shall pass away, but my words shall not pass away. But of that day and hour knoweth no man, no, not the angels of heaven, but my Father only." This answer by Christ refers to a time at least a thousand years after the Apocalypse, the time of that great battle of Armageddon. It does not refer to the time of Armageddon. As these two verses explain; no one knows that exact time; but an entry in the Book of Daniel gives an approximation of that end time. It incorporates that thousand year Millennium period.

In Daniel, Chapter 12, verse 6, one asked the question, "How long shall it be to the end of these wonders? Verse 7 gives the full answer:

"And I heard the man clothed in linen, which was upon the waters of the river, (the flow of humanity) when he held up his right hand and his left hand unto heaven, and sware by him that liveth for ever that it shall be for a time, times, and an half; and when he shall have accomplished to scatter the power of the holy people, all these things shall be finished." Then there are clues in Daniel and Revelation that give the length of this 'time, times, and an half.'

Verse 11 of the same chapter gives the first clue, "And from the time that the daily sacrifice shall be taken away, and the abomination that maketh desolate set up, there shall be a thousand two hundred and ninety days." That computes to three and a half years, which would be: time is one year, times would be two years, half a time would be half a year. By using that formula, and by considering the time of the millennium, that answer to Daniel would be approximately 3500 years. It must be remembered that this question was asked 500 BC, during Daniel's time.

Revelation, Chapter 12, gives more clues to understand this 'time, times, and half a time.' Verse 5 introduces a 'man child caught up unto God and to his throne.' This man child was from a 'woman' which refers to the coming religion of Christianity. Verse 6 continues, "And the woman fled into the wilderness, where she hath a place prepared of God, that they should feed her there a thousand two hundred and threescore days." Again, this is approximately three and a half years. This is the time Jesus was taken to Egypt after he was threatened to death by Herod. This is explained in verse 4. But, how is this time related to explain the time of the Apocalypse? Chapter 12 explains more.

Verse 14 says the woman (religion) was protected by 'two wings of a great eagle' where she is protected for a time, times, and half a time from the face of the serpent (Satan.) This was the time of acceptance of Christianity by Constantine the Great, and the Roman Catholic Church was formed approximately 350 AD. Christianity was then protected for a time, times, and half a time from Satan. This brings the time line to approximately 700 AD. This was the beginning of Islam created by Satan, which then revived the violent attacks against Christians and Jews. Now we ask, how is the time of the Battle of Armageddon considered? Considering all this information about times we merely subtract that thousand year millennium, and Daniel's time

-500 BC, from the 3500 years and we get approximately 2000 AD; the times of today. No one knows the exact 'day or hour.'

Why are the times not given in actual years? Because Daniel lived at a time before times were changed by the Julian calendar and the Gregorian calendar. And, Daniel would not have known the times of BC and AD. Since exact dates and times of other events such as the formal establishment of Islam could not be determined beforehand, there was no way for John of the Apocalypse to assign those exact dates. That explains the great importance of 'time, times, and half a time.'

So, when will the first bomb fall? The mathematical calculations suggest approximately April, 2019, which is 'time, times, and half a time' after the signing of the Iranian Nuclear Agreement; that JCPOA. That JCPOA is a critical time clue. Now, let's understand the importance of that Iran Agreement.

Chapter 1

Is the JCPOA the Time Clue?

This is a statement from the State Department regarding that Iran Nuclear Agreement:

"On July 14, 2015, the P5+1 (China, France, Germany, Russia, the United Kingdom, and the United States), the European Union (EU), and Iran reached a Joint Comprehensive Plan of Action (JCPOA) to ensure that Iran's nuclear program will be exclusively peaceful. October 18, 2015 marked Adoption Day of the JCPOA, the date on which the JCPOA came into effect and participants began taking steps necessary to implement their JCPOA commitments. January 16, 2016, marks Implementation Day of the JCPOA. The International Atomic Energy Agency (IAEA) has verified that Iran has implemented its key nuclear-related measures described in the JCPOA, and the Secretary State has confirmed the IAEA's verification. As a result of Iran verifiably meeting its nuclear commitments, the United States and the EU have lifted nuclear-related sanctions on Iran, as described in the JCPOA."

It's clear from this statement, and from date plans for many follow-on actions, that a time certain for implementation of the act is not established. There are many dates involved with this process. Why is this lack of a clear date implementation of the plan so important? It complicates the more specific time of 'time, times, and half a time.' That event, the direct attack against Israel, refers only to a general time. That information begins in Daniel, Chapter 9. It concerns a covenant; likely referring to that JCPOA.

Verse 27: "And he shall confirm the covenant with many for one week: (seven years) and in the midst of the week he shall cause the sacrifice and the oblation to cease, and for the overspreading of abominations he shall make it desolate, even until the consummation, and that determined shall be poured upon the desolate." Then Chapter 12, verse 11, adds a more specific time: "And from the time that the daily sacrifice shall be taken away, and the abomination that maketh desolate set up, there shall be a thousand two hundred and ninety days." Here is that three and a half years again, April, 2019 approximately three and a half years after that JCPOA agreement.

Plus, there's another time entry that corroborates this time approximate. Although these two times indicated are somewhat confusing, they relate to that time frame. It's given in verses 25-26:

"Know therefore and understand, that from the going forth of the commandment to restore and to build Jerusalem unto the Messiah the Prince shall be seven weeks, and threescore and two weeks: the street shall be built again, and the wall, even in troublous times. 26) And after threescore and two weeks shall Messiah be cut off, but not for himself: and the people of the prince that shall come shall destroy the city and the sanctuary; and the end thereof shall be with a flood, and unto the end of the war desolations are determined." Realize that the word Prince with the upper case P represents Christ. The prince with the lower case p represents Satan. Satan's forces, Islam, will come to destroy Jerusalem approximately three and a half years after that JCPOA agreement; and approximately seventy weeks after the decision to move the U.S. Embassy to Jerusalem.

But, what about the comment about the 'street' and the 'wall?' Could the 'wall' represent the renovated consulate building in Jerusalem that will become the new Embassy building? And, new street signs have just been placed on streets marking the location of the new Embassy. Ordinarily the 'wall' refers to the Western Wall of the Temple Mount in Jerusalem. On that Temple Mount is an Islamic abomination known as the Dome of the Rock. According to gotquestions.org, the Dome of the Rock is a Muslim shrine that was built on the Temple Mount in Jerusalem in AD 691. The Dome of the Rock is part of a larger Muslim holy area that takes up a significant portion of what is also known as Mount Moriah in the heart of Jerusalem. That abomination that causes desolation is already in place.

The 'wall' often refers to the Western Wall or the 'wailing wall.' That wall was liberated from the Islamic Palestinians and Jordanians as a result of the Six Day War. According to thekotel.org: "Until the Six Day War (in 1967, when Jerusalem was liberated), the Western Wall had no prayer plaza. There was just a narrow alleyway in the Muslim Mughrabi neighborhood - the Al-Buraq Alley, which was 28 meters long and only 3.6 meters wide. After the war and reunification of Jerusalem, the area was expanded. Today it is approximately 57 meters long and can accommodate up to 60,000 people. The Western Wall Plaza officially serves as a synagogue."

In the Bible, Daniel 9:27, it's written that a covenant by many to protect Israel will be abandoned in its 'midst,' and other words to the effect that Israel will be attacked. Later, in Matthew and Revelation, it's written that Israel will again be destroyed. Israel was destroyed twice in past history. In neither case was there a covenant or an agreement by many nations to protect Israel. It was first destroyed in 587 BC by Nebuchadnezzar, then by the Romans in 70 AD. This new Iranian Agreement was 'by many.' According to Daniel 9:27,

19

Jerusalem will be attacked in the 'midst' of that agreement; meaning possibly April, 2019. It will be a sudden and surprise attack.

Chapter 24 of Matthew gives many examples of reasons to flee when the sudden attack happens. For example, verse 17 reads, "Let him which is on the house top not come down to take any thing out of his house," flee to the mountains instead as admonished in verse 16. According to Revelation 16:15, "Behold, I come as a thief. Blessed is he that watcheth, and keepeth his garments, lest he walk naked, and they see his shame." Chapter 22, verse 7 adds, "Behold, I come quickly; blessed is he that keepeth the sayings of the prophesy of this book."

According to these warnings and admonitions, can we afford not to consider that April, 2019 date as the date to be prepared for the time of tribulation; and according to Matthew, the beginning of that time of horrors?

Chapter 2

What is the Tribulation?

This tribulation as mentioned in Daniel and Revelation refers to a time of great hardship and horror for Christians and Jews. And, as mentioned earlier, this approximate time is focused around certain detailed events. This tribulation period is generally accepted by most Christians as the time of great hardship for a period of seven years. Many believe it will be led by the Antichrist and will end with the return of Jesus to win the battle of Good over Evil. And, many believe there will be a period of 'Rapture' before the great retribution begins so Christians will not have to suffer the persecution by that Antichrist and his band of evil angels.

If this belief were true then there would be no beheadings and physical horrors against Christians. Only those who would not accept that 'Mark of the Beast' would suffer those horrible consequences. In reality, this is not the case at all; not even close. The revealed story is that the world has already entered the beginning of tribulation; and that great tribulation will begin when the first bomb falls on Israel, possibly in April, 2019. That's three and a half years after the countdown from that covenant began. The word 'Rapture' does not exist in the Bible; neither does the idea that Christians will escape those horrors.

What Revelation reveals is that those who are killed, martyred, during the tribulation period will not have to be reviewed later in the 'Book of Life.' They will reign with Christ in Heaven during the Millennium period, that thousand years after Armageddon. This information begins in Chapter 6, verse 9, when the fifth seal was opened:

"And when he had opened the fifth seal, I saw under the altar the souls of them that were slain for the word of God, and for the testimony which they held: 10) And they cried with a loud voice, saying, How long, O Lord, holy and true, dost thou not judge and avenge our blood on them that dwell on the earth? 11) And white robes were given unto every one of them; and it was said unto them, that they should rest yet for a little season, until their fellowservants also and their brethren that should be killed as they were, should be fulfilled."

But, what about those who were to be killed while their fellowservants waited for their turn to be judged for eternal salvation. This next piece of information is presented in Chapter 13, verse 15:

"And he had power to give life unto the image of the beast, that the image of the beast should both speak, and cause that as many as would not worship the image of the beast should be killed."

To understand who this person 'he' is it's first necessary to know the three beasts of Revelation. The word 'beast' is used many times in Revelation, but in many cases these describe a message or an event that portrays an action; such as the four 'beasts' who introduced the four horses of the Apocalypse. The three real beasts, however, are real beasts with names. Chapter 13 begins by describing a beast with seven heads rising up out of the sea. This beast represents the totality of Islam which has now spread to seven continents - thereby seven heads. This beast, Islam, is defined in Chapter 17 as 'Mystery Babylon the Great, the Mother of Harlots and Abominations of the Earth. Verse 6 makes the specific and definitive identification:

"And I saw the woman drunken with the blood of the saints and with the blood of the martyrs of Jesus." What other religion on the seven continents is 'drunken with the blood of the saints and with the blood of the martyrs of Jesus' other than Islam? More information in Chapter 17 and Chapter 12 also confirms this identification of Islam. Now let's return to understand who will 'give life unto the image of the beast' as detailed above in Chapter 13, verse 15. To understand the identity of this beast however, we must understand who was the first beast; also known as the Antichrist. This begins in Chapter 13, verse 3:

"And I saw one of his heads as it were wounded to death; and his deadly wound was healed; and all the world wondered after the beast." This describes Muhammad, and his wound at the Battle of Uhud. This was a battle between Meccans and early Muslims in 624 AD. In that battle, Muhammad was wounded in the head by arrows and smashed in the mouth with rocks. When he fell as dead, his troops left the battle and retreated to a hill in the rear. Later, Muhammad rose as from the dead and joined them in retreat. Verse 5 adds more information that clearly identifies Muhammad as that first beast:

"And there was given unto him a mouth speaking great things and blasphemies; and power was given unto him to continue forty and two months." This is that time of three and a half years again. In this case Muhammad was poisoned by a Jewish woman, in 628 AD, who was forced to cook for Muhammad and some of his troops after one of his battles. She sneaked poison into the meal whereby most of the troops were killed. Muhammad survived and 'continued' forty two months until he died in 632. Then verse 6 relates Muhammad's great blasphemy against Christ. He claimed to be higher on God's order than Jesus Christ. This is the maximum blasphemy:

"And he opened his mouth in blasphemy against God, to blaspheme his name, and his tabernacle, and them that dwell in heaven." Verse 10 then gives an analogy of Muhammad's death, "He that leadeth into captivity shall go into captivity: he that killeth with the sword must be killed with the sword. Here is the patience and the faith of the saints." The next verses, beginning with 11, then announce and describe the second beast, also known as the false prophet:

"And I beheld another beast coming up out of the earth; and he had two horns like a lamb, and he spake as a dragon." In other words, he claimed to be a Christian but he spoke positively only the words of that dragon, Satan, the god of Islam. Verse 12 continues:

"And he exerciseth all the power of the first beast before him, and causeth the earth and them which dwell therein to worship the first beast, whose deadly wound was healed." The first beast, Muhammad had the power as the leader of a nation. The second beast had that same power as the leader of a nation. As the leader of a nation with a worldwide voice, he influenced many to respect and accept that satanic voice of Islam. Verse 13 continues with more information to help identify this false prophet deceiver:

"And he doeth great wonders, so that he maketh fire come down from heaven on the earth in the sight of men." As Apostle John described this vision he had no words to describe aircraft and aerial combat; fire from the sky. How could he describe the fire power of aircraft during his time two thousand years ago. Even if he could have described it it would have voided his information until the twentieth century. His readers before that time would have thought he was having crazy fantasies; big metal objects flying in the sky! However, this modern day false prophet used the deception of air power to fulfill one of his missions assigned by Satan. One of those assigned tasks was to create that 'image to the beast.' This explanation begins in verse 14:

"And he deceiveth them that dwell on the earth by the means of those miracles which he had power to do in the sight of the beast; saying to them that dwell on the earth, that they should make an image to the beast, which had the wound by a sword, and did live."

Simply stated in modern terms; he allowed that image to the beast to be created, that ISIS caliphate, by meekly pretending to repel that group by timid air power. In his own words to deceive, he, Barack Hussein Obama, dismissed ISIS as a "JV" team, suggesting they weren't to be taken seriously in their attempt to create that 'image to the beast.' Then verse 15 begins the introduction of the tribulation. This is not the 'great tribulation' for it's confined to that area of the Middle East. It involves great peril and horrors to those in that area who refuse to follow the demands of that caliphate, that image to the beast:

"And he had power to give life unto the image of the beast, that the image of the beast should both speak and cause that as many as would not worship the image of the beast should be killed. 16) And he causeth all, both small and great, rich and poor, free and bond, to receive a mark in their right hand, or in their foreheads: 17) And that no man might buy or sell, save he that had the mark, or the name of the beast or the number of his name." (Note that he caused this to happen; he did not personally make it happen.) Is there any doubt that those who worship God, living under these horrible conditions, this time of horrors, have a serious decision to make? They must either accept that mark of the beast (the acceptance of Islam in their foreheads, or to fight for Islam by holding weapons in their hands) or they must accept death. Certainly those who choose death to follow Christ are those chosen for that first resurrection to rule with Christ during that thousand years before the second resurrection. Then verse 18 gives the identity of this man who follows Satan's will by deception:

25

"Here is wisdom. Let him that hath understanding count the number of the beast; (this second beast) for it is the number of a man; and his number is Six hundred threescore and six." (666) By counting this number 6+6+6 the result is 18, which is the number of letters in the man's name. One man of today fulfills the descriptions in all these verses: BARACKHUSSEINOBAMA. Apostle John also gave us a password to confirm this number. The password is that this name is identified in VERSE 18.

So, when will the 'great' tribulation begin? It begins when Islam, likely Iran, drops the first nuclear bomb on Israel. My calculations suggest that will be approximately April, 2019. This war activity is described as the seven trumpets are blown by the seven angels. Opening of the seventh seal introduces these trumpets. Before we review the activity announced by those trumpets, let's first explore the information presented when the seven seals are opened.

Chapter 3

The Seven Seals

The seven seals introduced in Revelation, Chapter 5, act as a table of contents of things to come related to the real beasts, Armageddon, and the end of times. Before those seals are opened, as described in following chapters, Chapter 4 gives the validity of the information exposed when those seals are opened. Verses 6-8 detail the 'crystal clear' source of that information:

"And before the throne there was a sea of glass like unto crystal: and in the midst of the throne, and round about the throne, were four beasts full of eyes before and behind. 7) And the first beast was like a lion, and the second beast like a calf, and the third beast had a face as a man, and the fourth beast was like a flying eagle. 8) And the four beasts had each of them six wings about him; and they were full of eyes within: and they rest not day and night..." More simply stated; these four 'beasts' could see everything crystal clear, in the future and in the past. And, they never rested from their high worldly observations. Perhaps this is the source of our current comment of 'it's crystal clear.'

Then Chapter 5 gives the source of those seven seals. It begins:

"And I saw in the right hand of him that sat on the throne a book written within and on the backside, sealed with seven seals." There was despair because the angels around the throne searched for someone 'worthy' to open the seals. Then verse 5 explains who was capable of opening the seven seals:

"And one of the elders saith unto me, Weep not: behold, the Lion of Juda, the Root of David, hath prevailed to open the book, and to loose the seven seals thereof." Verse 9 explains their joy when one was chosen to open those seals:

"And they sung a new song, saying, Thou art worthy to take the book and to open the seals thereof: for thou wast slain, and hast redeemed us to God by they blood out of every kindred, and tongue, and people and nation." Verse 12 adds, "Saying with a loud voice, Worthy is the Lamb that was slain to receive power, and riches, and wisdom, and strength, and honor, and glory, and blessings." Then Chapter 6 begins the information within those seven seals. The first four seals introduced by those four beasts 'full of eyes within' revealed the 'four horses of the Apocalypse.' Chapter 6 begins:

"And I saw when the Lamb opened one of the seals, and I heard, as it were the noise of thunder, one of the four beasts saying, Come and see." This was the first beast described 'as a lion.' Verse 2 then describes what John saw. "And I saw, and behold a white horse: and he that sat on him had a bow; and he went forth conquering, and to conquer." The information in this verse is usually interpreted as Satan going forth to conquer. This common interpretation is erroneous. This is the prophesy, that view from the beast with many eyes before and behind, that Christ will go forth to conquer and eventually destroy Satan and his followers. Two items confirm this interpretation. First, this view is presented by the beast 'like a lion.' The lion represents

Christ; the lion of Juda. Second, only Christ rides a white horse and goes forth to conquer. Satan is never described as 'conquering.'

In verse 3 the second beast, the one like a calf, responds to opening of the second seal, "And when he had opened the second seal, I heard the second beast say, Come and see. 4) And there went out another horse that was red: and power was given to him that sat thereon to take peace from the earth, and that they should kill one another: and there was given unto him a great sword." This red horse describes Satan. The rider is a description of Islam, who will 'kill one another.' As the analogy of the beast like a calf; he will be slaughtered like a calf.

Islam, as one, has two parts; the Shiite and the Sunni. They don't hesitate to 'kill one another.' This concept is explained further in two other places. First is in John's letter to the church at Thyatira where he describes that Jezebel who calls herself a prophetess. This is an analogy of the Mother of Harlots described in Chapter 17. In other words, it describes Islam. In verse 23 of Chapter 2 it states, "And I will kill her children with death." Second, then verses in Chapter 17 explain how these two things will happen; God will kill her children with death, and that one rider of the red horse will kill one another. It's the same action. It begins in verse 16:

"And the ten horns which thou sawest upon the beast, these shall hate the whore, and shall make her desolate and naked, and shall eat her flesh, and burn her with fire. 17) For God hath put in their hearts to fulfill his will, and to agree, and give their kingdom unto the beast until the words of God shall be fulfilled." In other words, God will kill Jezebel's children with death by allowing the rider of the red horse, Islam, to kill one another. The ten formal Islamic nations will kill those harlot radicals; otherwise known as terrorists.

29

Opening of the third seal takes a more earthly view, beginning with verse 5, "And when he had opened the third seal, I heard the third beast say, Come and see. And I beheld, and lo a black horse; and he that sat on him had a pair of balances in his hand. 6) And I heard a voice in the midst of the four beasts say, A measure of wheat for a penny, and three measures of barley for a penny; and see thou hurt not the oil and the wine." As described earlier, this third beast had the face of a man; an earthly personification.

Going forth of this black horse, introduced by the beast having 'a face as a man' is explained later in Revelation. It suggests sustenance and other daily survival problems of people as they seek food and water to maintain life during the deepest part of the tribulation. Shortage or absence of these items will be worldwide when the great tribulation begins. Why will this worldwide shortage exist? It will happen mostly from two reasons. First, there is now such dependence on globalization and world trade that many items will not be manufactured. Secondly, as explained later in Revelation, there will be no or limited 'ships on the sea.' Likely this would also include those ships known as trucks and carriers on roads and highways. Lack of gasoline and acts of terrorism by Islamists would also limit that capacity. Perhaps many of those pre-positioned warriors are already in place ready to fulfill that 'glorious' mission that sends them to paradise.

The fourth beast, that 'was like a flying eagle' had a different mission to introduce as he said Come and see, when the fourth seal was opened. Verse 8 continues, "And I looked, and behold a pale horse and his name that sat on him was Death, and Hell followed with him. And power was given unto them over the fourth part of the earth, to kill with sword, and with hunger, and with death, and with the beasts of the earth." This explains most of the natural deaths that will occur from everyday living. And, those beasts of the earth do not include beasts such as lions and tigers.

The paleness of this horse refers to the horror and despair of dying from natural causes such as heart attacks, cancer, diabetes and other deaths that ordinarily could be reduced or ameliorated with medicines or other treatments. Conflicts from ordinary daily survival such as fighting for food by desperate and starving people would cause 'death by the sword.' And we should not forget those beasts of the earth.

These beasts would refer to germs, insects and parasites that ordinarily can be controlled by insecticides and other eradicators. The hoards of mosquitoes would increase as well as ticks and other parasites that would increase due to the lack of flora maintenance. Most emphasis would be on finding a food and water source, not on maintaining beautiful highways, byways and parks. This pale horse represents the natural deaths that occur when effective preventions are not maintained.

This fourth beast that introduced the fourth horse of the Apocalypse was the last beast to make an introduction when a seal was opened. The remaining seals were introduced without that special attention. Chapter 6, verse 9 begins the results of opening the fifth seal:

"And when he had opened the fifth seal, I saw under the altar the souls of them that were slain for the word of God, and for the testimony which they held. 10) And they cried with a loud voice, saying, How long, O Lord, holy and true, dost thou not judge and avenge our blood on them that dwell on the earth?" In response they were told to be patient 'yet for a little season, until their fellowservants also and their bretheren, that should be killed as they were, should be fulfilled.' These were the souls of those who had been killed before the period of tribulation. Their plea was answered after that great battle in which that Babylon the Great, Islam, was destroyed. That's stated in Chapter 19, beginning with the first verse:

"And after these things I heard a great voice of much people in heaven, saying, Alleluia; Salvation, and glory, and honour, and power, unto the Lord our God; 2) For true and righteous are his judgments: for he hath judged the great whore, which did corrupt the earth with her fornication, and hath avenged the blood of his servants at her hand."

Opening of the sixth seal, detailed in Chapter 6, verse 12, revealed the beginning of great disasters upon the earth. "And I beheld when he had opened the sixth seal, and, lo, there was a great earthquake; and the sun became black as sackcloth of hair, and the moon became as blood 13) and the stars of heaven fell unto the earth, even as a fig tree casteth her untimely figs, when she is shaken of a mighty wind."

The next verses give more information of great disasters to occur ever to the point of the enemy asking to be hidden in falling rocks from the wrath of the Lamb. It concludes with verse17, "For the great day of his wrath is come; and who shall be able to stand?" Before the results of opening that seventh seal are revealed there is a pause described in Chapter 7.

Chapter 7 describes a pause in coming warfare activities until certain people are allowed to be saved; and for 144,000 Jews to accept God's salvation through the Lamb. They will accept Christ as their Savior Plus there will be many more converts. A statement is also made about damage to the planet through these warfare activities. This is reflected in verses 2-3:

"And I saw another angel ascending from the east, having the seal of the living God: and he cried with a loud voice to the four angels, to whom it was given to hurt the earth and the sea, 3) Saying, Hurt not the earth, neither the sea, nor the trees, till we have sealed the servant of our God in their foreheads." Verse 4 adds even more, "And I heard the number of them which were sealed: and there were sealed a hundred and forty and four thousand of all the the tribes of the children of Israel." Chapter 7 concludes that those who accept God through the Lamb will be comforted and protected. The last two verses explain:

"They shall hunger no more, neither thirst any more; neither shall the sun light on them, nor any heat. 17) For the Lamb which is in the midst of the throne shall feed them, and shall lead them unto living fountains of waters: and God shall wipe away all tears from their eyes."

This information also gives a clue to that mark of the beast in the foreheads of those who accept that beast. That mark is not an actual mark; it's the acceptance of Satan through the conduit of Islam. That mark on the hand is an analogy that the hand will be used to enforce that mark of the beast; as Islamic terrorists are doing throughout the world today.

Finally that seventh seal is opened. That continues in Chapter 8 with an ominous foreboding:

"And when he had opened the seventh seal, there was silence in heaven about the space of half an hour. 2) And I saw the seven angels which stood before God; and to them were given seven trumpets. 3) And another angel came and stood at the altar, having a golden censer; and there was given unto him much incense, that he should offer it with the prayers of all saints upon the golden altar which was before the throne. 5) And the angel took the censer, and filled it with fire of the altar, and cast it into the earth: and there were voices, and thunderings, and lightnings, and an earthquake. 6) And the seven angels which had the seven trumpets prepared themselves to sound."

As each trumpet sounds it reveals a new warfare event or an event that notes time in a sequence of events. Those seven trumpets will be analysed next.

Chapter 4

The Seven Trumpets

Chapter 8, verse 7 reveals the sound of the first trumpet:

"The first angel sounded, and there followed hail and fire mingled with blood, and they were cast upon the earth: and the third part of trees was burnt up, and all green grass was burnt up."

This first trumpet announced the beginning of the great war that would evolve into that Battle of Armageddon. This will be the surprise attack 'as a thief in the night' warned about in Matthew, Chapter 24, and in several places in Revelation. Most certainly, this would be a nuclear attack on one major city, region or military base in Israel. That area would suffer from a loss of a third of the trees and all the grass; and that devastation would represent nuclear activity. As a great nuclear cloud rose high into the atmosphere might that not create frozen crystals that would turn into hail that would then fall back to earth, along with the blood of those who had been directly affected by that bomb? Where might this happen: Tel Aviv, Jerusalem, or on one or more major Israeli military facilities?

This could also involve a ground attack by rockets and artillery shells; which are presented as 'hail' in another verse in Revelation. This information is presented in Chapter 16, verse 21:

"And there fell upon men a great hail out of heaven, every stone about the weight of a talent: and men blasphemed God because of the plague of the hail; for the hail thereof was exceeding great." At that time a Greek talent was 82 pounds in silver and double that in gold. In this case, Apostle John was describing missiles or rockets, not actual hail. He had never known the words for rockets and artillery shells.

Verse 8 then announces the results from the sound of the second trumpet, "And the second angel sounded, and as it were a great mountain burning with fire was cast into the sea; and the third part of the sea became blood; 9) And the third part of the creatures which were in the sea, and had life, died; and the third part of the ships were destroyed."

This obviously describes what John saw in his vision as the second nuclear bomb struck a large facility near a seaport. This bomb not only killed people, but it also killed many animals in the sea as it destroyed a major target; those ships in that seaport. This target obviously was to eliminate resupply and support to the defensive organizations in Israel. This would add more limitations to that normally provided by air support.

The sound of the third trumpet introduced something entirely different from a war related event. This was a time clue event; something which would be related to a time when that sudden attack by Islam would occur. It begins in verse 10:

"And the third angel sounded, and there fell a great star from heaven burning as it were a lamp, and it fell upon the third part of the rivers and upon the fountains of waters; 11) And the name of the star is called Wormwood: and the third part of the waters became wormwood; and many men died of the waters, because they were made bitter." So, what is a star named Wormwood?

Wormwood is not a celestial star. Star is simply a word that represents a major event that has happened in our current time. That event is drug and opioid abuse. Wormwood is the name of a bitter plant that grows wild across many nations. It's also the source of the bitter drink absinthe; and is the source of an artificial cannabis substance. In effect, this star Wormwood is a word that represents a major drug and substance abuse crisis in the world at approximately the same time as the bombs dropping on Israel. This article from the New York Times, Jan. 6, 2017, titled, 'Inside a Killer Drug Epidemic: A Look at America's Opioid Crisis' gives an example of the spread of this drug crisis; this Wormwood:

"The opioid epidemic killed more than 33,000 people in 2015. What follows are stories of a national affliction that has swept the country, from cities on the West Coast to bedroom communities in the Northeast.

Opioid addiction is America's 50-state epidemic. It courses along Interstate highways in the form of cheap smuggled heroin, and flows out of "pill mill" clinics where pain medicine is handed out like candy. It has ripped through New England towns, where people overdose in the aisles of dollar stores, and it has ravaged coal country, where addicts speed-dial the sole doctor in town licensed to prescribe a medication.

Public health officials have called the current opioid epidemic the worst drug crisis in American history, killing more than 33,000 people in 2015. Overdose deaths were nearly equal to the number of deaths from car crashes. In 2015, for the first time, deaths from heroin alone surpassed gun homicides.

And there's no sign it's letting up, a team of New York Times reporters found as they examined the epidemic on the ground in states across the country. From New England to "safe injection" areas in the Pacific Northwest, communities are searching for a way out of a problem that can feel inescapable." End of article.

Drug and opioid abuse is a great problem today across the world. What other purpose would Christ have to give this information for Apostle John to write other than to relate the time of that coming great battle to a major and active world event that can be seen and understood? This is the major time clue of coming great horrors. The words about 'burning as it were a lamp' refer to bongs which are used to increase the intensity of some drugs. Now let's move on to that fourth trumpet

Verse 12 describes many dark and foreboding activities of darkness from the sun, moon and stars. Verse 13 then gives the warning of worse horrors coming; even to the extreme of calling them woes:

"And I beheld, and heard an angel flying through the midst of heaven saying with a loud voice, Woe, woe, woe, to the inhabiters of the earth by reason of the other voices of the trumpets of the three angels, which are yet to sound!

Chapter 9 then reveals what happened when trumpets five and six were sounded. It begins with the fifth trumpet. "And the fifth angel sounded, and I saw a star fall from heaven unto the earth: and to him was given the key of the bottomless pit. 2) And he opened the bottomless pit; and there arose a smoke out of the pit, as the smoke of a great furnace; and the sun and the air were darkened by reason of the smoke of the pit. 3) And there came out of the smoke locusts upon the earth: and unto them was given power, as the scorpions of the earth have power." Although this seems something from a Star Wars fantasy, a simple interpretation gives this vision more real life.

This star was the announcement or the introduction of an event. That event was warfare. The key was 'of' the beginning of warfare, not the key 'to' open a great pit in the ground. And, most likely, this was the vision of a ground battle that will happen after that sudden nuclear attack against Israel. The next several verses give interpretations and descriptions of the battlefield as Apostle John visualized. Although many interpret this chapter explaining the events when that fifth trumpet sounded as an attack by Satan, this is not the correct interpretation. This chapter explains God's forces destroying those forces of Satan. Verse 4 explains:

"And it was commanded them that they should not hurt the grass of the earth, neither any green thing, neither any tree; but only those men which have not the seal of God in their foreheads." This information is very clear. These attacks will be against those who wish to destroy God and his followers. Furthermore, if these were Satan's forces, Islam, they would have no concern about protecting anything in the environment, including fauna or flora. This one given the key 'of' the bottomless pit (warfare) is a representative of God's forces.

Verse 5 adds to the idea that this will be a limited battle for a limited purpose. The purpose likely is to destroy the economic source of Satan's forces, which is oil. The verse continues, "And to them it was given that they should not kill them, but that they should be tormented five months: and their torment was as the torment of a scorpion, when he striketh a man." Then the next few verses describe those 'beasts' on the battlefield: scorpions, locusts, things having teeth as the teeth of lions, and those having hair as the hair of women.

These are not the current-day names of these unbelievable warriors. These names merely describe aircraft on the horizon that first appear as a swarm of locusts; helicopters that have the general appearance of scorpions, and grills of armoured vehicles that appear as the teeth of lions. I recognized these analogies on the flightline when I served in Vietnam in 1966.

And what about those that had 'hair as the hair of women?' These really are women who now serve on the front lines of our battlefields and in the air; with helmets on their heads as 'crowns of gold.' These are the things that make great graphics, but these graphical representations are false. These are real people using modern-day weaponry. If John had written the actual identities of these weapons no one would have understood; and John's writings likely would have been discredited and discarded as a science fiction novel. Perhaps that's why Christ did not give John the names of these things.

After these descriptions, verse 11 then identifies the leader of these forces, "And they had a king over them, which is the angel of the bottomless pit, whose name in the Hebrew tongue is Abaddon, but in the Greek tongue hath his name Apollyon." These names are generally interpreted as 'Destruction' or 'Destroyer,' and most interpreters suggest this is Satan or one of Satan's angels. But, this could not be true since they are instructed not to harm anyone who 'has the seal of God in their foreheads.'

This person is identified as a king, which would mean he is the leader of a nation. At this moment in time, and given the current event taking place especially in the Middle East, this king who will lead this attack against Satan's forces on the battlefield could be none other than President Donald Trump. Thus far he has demonstrated positive resolve to thwart Satan's forces; especially with his attacks against Syria when Syria used chemical warfare against so many of its innocent citizens. Who else has shown this resolve to defend humanity; through the Spirit of Christ? Donald Trump has been challenged and he met that challenge. He will be challenged again; and again he will lead God's forces to prevail again in an even greater battle.

Verse 12 concludes, "One woe is past, and, behold, there come two woes more hereafter." Verse 13 then announces the continuation and broadening of that war, "And the sixth angel sounded, and I heard a voice from the four horns of the golden altar which is before God, 14) Saying to the sixth angel which had the trumpet, Loose the four angels which are bound in the great river Euphrates. 15) And the four angels were loosed, which were prepared for an hour, and a day, and a month, and a year, for to slay the third part of men."

This battle would last over a year and would involve many forces, even those outside the Middle East, as suggested by easy passage across what had been large waters that separated the other regions of Asia. Verse 16 continues to demonstrate the numbers of warriors involved:

"And the number of the army of the horsemen were two hundred thousand thousand: and I heard the number of them. 17) And thus I saw the horses in the vision, and them that sat on them, having breastplates of fire, and of jacinth, and brimstone: and the heads of the horses were as the heads of lions; and out of their mouths issued fire and smoke and brimstone. 18) By these three was the third part of men killed, by the fire, and by the smoke, and by the brimstone, which issued out of their mouths. 19) For their power is in their mouths, and in their tails: for their tails were like unto serpents, and had heads, and with them they do hurt."

Two considerations are involved in these verses. First, what are these horses having breastplates of fire, and of jacinth, and brimstone? John didn't know the modern name of a military tank, so he called them horses. What else could he say when he visualized them? These new

41

tanks can run as fast as a horse, and they can reverse their tubular cannons front to rear; which would make it appear to John that they could issue fire from their mouths and their tails; that were as long as a serpent.

The other consideration is the number of two hundred million men Where did they come from? What area could produce an army that size? The answer: China. An article at this link provides that information:

http://foreignpolicy.com/2018/05/16/on-chinas-new-silk-road-democracy-pays-a-toll/

This is part of that longer article that explains China's new silk road program. It's designed to return China to its once greatness in that region. Iran and Israel play a large role in providing natural gas and oil resources in the long range plans of China to become the dominate force in Eurasia, as well as the rest of the world. When war begins in that area China cannot afford to sit idly by and watch its plans of long term existence be destroyed. This is the introduction to that article:

"Great power competition is back. And China is now combining it vast economic resources with a muscular presence on the global stage One of Beijing's key efforts is the Belt and Road Initiative, a trillion dollar endeavor to link together Asia, the Middle East, Africa, and Europe through a web of mostly Chinese-funded physical and digital infrastructure.

Much of Washington has fretted over China's mercantilist approach to economics in general and views the Belt and Road Initiative largely through this lens. Yet the concerns over Beijing's current approach should go beyond dollars and yuan. By fueling debt dependency advancing a "China First" development model, and undermining good governance and human rights, the initiative offers a deeply illiberal approach to regions that contain about 65 percent of the world's population and one-third of its economic output.

The hype surrounding the Belt and Road Initiative — Chinese President Xi Jinping's signature initiative on the world stage — has recently shifted into overdrive. In China's domestic politics, support for the project has come to signify loyalty to the country's president-for-life. At the same time, the Belt and Road serves as an overarching narrative into which Beijing can fit its foreign economic policy in regions as disparate as the Arctic and Latin America. Yet the initiative's rhetoric and branding should not obscure its core aim: to access markets and project influence and power throughout Eurasia and the Indian Ocean rim. And China has already dedicated significant resources to the effort: Estimates put total Belt and Road-related construction and investment at more than $340 billion from 2014 to 2017."

China could easily produce a two hundred million man army from its three billion population. In fact, China might see a reduction in its population as a positive event, as they try to reduce population now by limiting the size of families.

Continuing in Chapter 9, verse 20 explains what happens to those who are not killed in this great battle, "And the rest of the men which were not killed by these plagues yet repented not of the works of their hands, that they should not worship devils, and idols of gold, and silver, and brass, and stone, and of wood; which neither can see, nor hear, nor walk." So, what is this idol of worship that can neither see, nor hear, nor walk? The common name is the Kaaba, and it's located in Mecca. It's made of those elements described above. This link provides more information about that site:

43

http://www.ibtimes.com/what-kaaba-black-cube-marking-islams
most-sacred-site-sparks-curiosity-1699203

"Every year millions of Muslims travel to Mecca for the hajj, one o
the five pillars of Islam. Muslims travel to Islam's most sacred
mosque, al-Masjid al-Haram, during the six-day pilgrimage. Mecca i
thought to be the place where Ishmael and his mother Hagar wer
provided with a spring of water in the desert. As it is the most sacred
place in Islam, non-Muslims are forbidden from entering.

In the center of the mosque, there is a black, box-shaped building
which has sparked questions from those unfamiliar with the Islami
culture. Here is everything to know about the most sacred space in th
Muslim world.

The Kaaba is built around a sacred black stone, a meteorite tha
Muslims believe was placed by Abraham and Ishmael in a corner o
the Kaaba, a symbol of God's covenant with Abraham and Ishmae
and, by extension, with the Muslim community itself. It is embedde
in the eastern corner of the Kaaba.

Muslims believe the Kaaba was originally built by Abraham an
Ishmael, but the site was re-dedicated by Muhammad and has bee
reconstructed since. When Muslims pray, wherever they are, they tur
toward the Kaaba, and during the hajj, pilgrims walk counterclockwis
around it seven times.

The Kaaba is made of granite from the hills near Mecca. The structur
is 50 feet high (15.24 meters), 35 feet (10.67 meters) wide and 40 fee
long (12.19 meters) long. Inside the Kaaba, the floor is made of marbl
and limestone. The interior walls, measuring 43 feet (13 meters) by 3
feet (9 meters), are clad with tiled, white marble halfway to the roo
with darker trimmings along the floor. It is covered by a black sil

cloth decorated with gold-embroidered calligraphy. This cloth is known as the kiswa, and it is replaced yearly."

Verse 21 adds, "Neither repented they of their murders, nor of their sorceries, nor of their fornication, nor of their thefts."

This second woe from the trumpet of the sixth angel then takes an unusual turn and is unclear, but it seems to suggest a truce or an agreement to halt the war. Chapter 11 begins:

"And there was given me a reed like unto a rod: and the angel stood, saying, Rise, and measure the temple of God, and the altar, and them that worship therein. 2) But the court which is without the temple leave out, and measure it not; for it is given unto the Gentiles: and the holy city shall they tread under foot forty and two months (three and a half years.) 3) And I will give power unto my two witnesses, and they shall prophesy a thousand two hundred and threescore days, clothed in sackcloth. 4) These are the two olive trees, and the two candlesticks standing before the God of the earth."

According to Chapter 2, verse 20, these two candlesticks represent two churches of God. Perhaps during this military pause these two churches that remain in Jerusalem would be the Protestant and Catholic representations. Then the next verses in Chapter 11 read that these two would have power over the rain and turning waters to blood. This rain refers to artillery shells and missiles; the waters refer to humanity. In other words they would represent military forces. The verses continue to explain that when their influence was over they would be attacked and killed by the 'beast that ascendeth out of the bottomless pit (bottomless pit refers to warfare) who shall make war against, them.'

Verses 9 and 10 then explain that their bodies will remain in the street
for three and a half days while those who killed them 'shall rejoic
over them, and make merry, and shall send gifts one to another
because these two prophets tormented them that dwell on the earth.
Verse 11 adds, "And after three days and an half the Spirit of life from
God entered into them, and they stood upon their feet; and great fea
fell upon them which saw them." Perhaps this means the Spirit of Go
replaced those fallen ones with others who would act in their place t
destroy those who had killed those 'two prophets.' Verse 13 describe
this new war activity:

"And the same hour was there a great earthquake, and the tenth part o
the city fell, and in the earthquake were slain of men seven thousand
and the remnant were affrighted, and gave glory to the God o
heaven." The remainder of Chapter 11 then explains what's to come
Verse 15 begins the sound of the seventh angel - that third woe:

"And the seventh angel sounded; and there were great voices i
heaven, saying, The kingdoms of the world are become the kingdom
of our Lord, and of his Christ; and he shall reign for ever and ever.
Then verses 18-19 give an introduction of worse things to come for th
beast and his followers:

"And the nations were angry, and thy wrath is come, and the time c
the dead, that they should be judged, and that thou shouldest giv
reward unto thy servants the prophets, and to the saints, and them tha
fear thy name, small and great; and shouldest destroy them whic
destroy the earth. 19) And the temple of God was opened in heaver
and there was seen in his temple the ark of his testament; and ther
were lightnings, and voices, and thunderings, and an earthquake, an
great hail."

Chapter 5

The Battle Continues

These battles and signs of battles during this war are presented in Revelation in no particular order, and are not easily discernable. Each part or presentation seems to be from a different view, or a different vision. Nevertheless, we will try to connect them in some way in some reasonable order. The next view of a major battle, possibly that Battle of Armageddon, comes from Chapter 14. It begins:

"And I looked, and , lo, a Lamb stood on the mount Sion, and with him and hundred forty and four thousand, having his Father's name written in their foreheads. Verse 7 then indicated the time of judgment from an angel's voice:

"Saying with a loud voice, Fear God, and give glory to him; for the hour of his judgment is come: and worship him that made heaven, and earth, and the sea, and the fountains of waters. 8) And there followed another angel, saying, Babylon is fallen, is fallen, that great city, because she made all nations drink of the wine of the wrath of her fornication. 9) And the third angel followed them, saying with a loud voice, If any man worship the beast and his image, and receive his mark in his forehead, or in his hand, 10) The same shall drink of the wine of the wrath of God, which is poured out without mixture into the cup of his indignation; and he shall be tormented with fire and brimstone in the presence of the holy angels, and in the presence of the Lamb."

Verse 11 then explains the result of the coming battle for those who worship the beast when they are killed, "And the smoke of their torment ascendeth up for ever and ever: and they have no rest day no night, who worship the beast and his image, and whosoever receiveth the mark of his name." The last verses, beginning with verse 14 then describe the two armies that will be formed by two angels using sickles:

"And I looked, and behold a white cloud, and upon the cloud one sat like unto the Son of man, having on his head a golden crown, and in his hand a sharp sickle. 15) And another angel came out of the temple crying with a loud voice to him that sat on the cloud, Thrust in th sickle, and reap: for the time is come for thee to reap; for the harvest of the earth is ripe. 16) And he that sat on the cloud thrust in his sickle on the earth; and the earth was reaped." This was a description of God gathering his forces for the battle. The choice by the other side begins in verse 17:

"And another angel came out of the temple which is in heaven, he also having a sharp sickle. 18) And another angel came out from the altar which had power over fire; and cried with a loud cry to him that had the sharp sickle, saying, Thrust in they sharp sickle, and gather the cluster of the vine of the earth; for her grapes are fully ripe. 19) And the angel thrust in his sickle into the earth, and gathered the vine of the earth, and cast it into the great winepress of the wrath of God." Verse 20 explains the conclusion when these two forces met:

"And the winepress was trodden without the city, and blood came out of the winepress, even unto the horse bridles, by the space of a thousand and six hundred furlongs." (A furlong is generally considered one-eighth of a mile or 220 yards.) This was a quick view of a battle, or part of a battle. Chapter 15 then introduces seven angels with seven vials of wrath. It begins:

"And I saw another sign in heaven, great and marvelous, seven angels having the seven last plagues; for in them is filled up the wrath of God. 6) And the seven angels came out of the temple, having the seven plagues, clothed in pure and white linen, and having their breasts girded with golden girdles. 7) and one of the four beasts gave unto the seven angels seven golden vials full of the wrath of God, who liveth for ever and ever." Then verse 8 concludes that the temple will be abandoned until the wrath of God from these seven vials is fulfilled.

As you read the results from these seven vials being poured out, consider that the individual results are connected to the actions from the specific sounds of those seven trumpets. This information about the vials begins in Chapter 16:

"And I heard a great voice out of the temple saying to the seven angels, Go your ways, and pour out the vials of the wrath of God upon the earth. 2) And the first went, and poured out his vial upon the earth; and there fell a noisome and grievous sore upon the men which had the mark of the beast, and upon them which worshipped his image. 3) And the second angel poured out his vial upon the sea; and it became as the blood of a dead man; and every living soul died in the sea." (This is when that mountain, that nuclear cloud, moved into a local sea.)

Verse 4 continues, "And the third angel poured out his vial upon the rivers and fountains of waters; and they became blood." This refers to humans and the flow of youth that continues that flow. Then the next verses explain this is justice because these who are killed, 6) "For they have shed the blood of saints and prophets, and thou hast given them blood to drink, for they are worthy." This describes those of Babylon

49

the Great defined in 17:6 as, "And I saw the woman drunken with the blood of the saints and with the blood of the martyrs of Jesus." This clearly defines Islam. Verse 8 continues with the fourth vial:

"And the fourth angel poured out his vial upon the sun; and power was given unto him to scorch men with fire. 9) And men were scorched with great heat, and blasphemed the name of God, which hath power over these plagues: and they repented not to give him glory. 10) And the fifth angel poured out his vial upon the seat of the beast; and his kingdom was full of darkness; and they gnawed their tongues for pain 11) And blasphemed the God of heaven because of their pains and their sores, and repented not of their deeds."

In verse 12 the sixth vial repeats information similar to that of the sixth trumpet, about the river Euphrates being dried up so the 'kings of the east might be prepared.' Verse 13 then describes the spirits of the dragon, Satan; and the beast, and the false prophet. As the 'spirits of devils, working miracles, which go forth unto the kings of the earth and of the whole world, to gather them to the battle of that great day of God Almighty.'

Verse 16 then gives that familiar warning to be prepared, "Behold, I come as a thief. Blessed is he that watcheth, and keepeth his garments, lest he walk naked, and they see his shame." The next verse then suggests the beginning of that Battle of Armageddon:

"And he gathered them together into a place called in the Hebrew tongue Armageddon." The remaining verses in this chapter give the results of that pouring from the seventh vial. This information is related to the information presented when the seventh trumpet was blown. Verse 17 continues:

"And the seventh angel poured out his vial into the air; and there came

50

a great voice out of the temple of heaven, from the throne, saying, It is done. 18) And there were voices, and thunders, and lightnings, and there was a great earthquake, such as was not since men were upon the earth, so mighty an earthquake, and so great. 19) And the great city was divided into three parts, and the cities of the nations fell: and great Babylon came in remembrance before God, to give unto her the cup of the wine of the fierceness of his wrath. 20) And every island fled away, and the mountains were not found. 21) and there fell upon men a great hail out of heaven, every stone about the weight of a talent: and men blasphemed God because of the plague of the hail; for the plague thereof was exceeding great."

Chapter 19 then gives a more spiritual view of the battle. It begins in verse 11:

"And I saw heaven opened, and behold a white horse; and he that sat upon him was called Faithful and True, and in righteousness he doth judge and make war. (This white horse was the same horse introduced by that first beast in Chapter 6.) 12) His eyes were as a flame of fire, and on his head were many crowns; and he had a name written, that no man knew, but he himself. 13) And he was clothed with a vesture dipped in blood: and his name is called The Word of God. 14) And the armies which were in heaven followed him upon white horses, clothed in fine linen, white and clean. 15) And out of his mouth goeth a sharp sword , that with it he should smite the nations: and he shall rule them with a rod of iron: and he treadeth the winepress of the fierceness and wrath of Almighty God." Clearly this 'sword' must be the Word of God fulfilled by the army of spirits within His physical warriors on earth. Verse 16 continues:

"And he hath on his vesture and on his thigh a name written, KING OF KINGS, AND LORD OF LORDS. 17) And I saw an angel standing in the sun: and he cried with a loud voice, saying to all the fowls that fly in the midst of heaven, Come and gather yourselve together unto the supper of the great God: 18) That ye may eat the flesh of kings, and the flesh of captains, and the flesh of mighty men and the flesh of horses, and of them that sit on them, and the flesh of all men, both free and bond, both small and great." The next verse then tell what happens when these armies meet:

And I saw the beast, and the kings of the earth, (these ten kings who represent the ten Islamic nations that will be involved) and their armie gathered together to make war against him that sat on the horse, an against his army. 20) And the beast was taken, (the spirit of th antichrist) and with him the false prophet that wrought miracles befor him, with which he deceived them that had received the mark of th beast, and them that worshipped his image. These both were cast aliv into a lake of fire burning with brimstone."

Perhaps in this case the second beast was not physically cast into the burning lake. Perhaps only the spirit of his influence on others wa destroyed so that he no longer could entice others to participate in th beast's plan to war against God. On the other hand, it's possible tha this false prophet might in some way participate in the planning an organizing of these warfare activities. We might not know an understand until that actually happens. Verse 20 then explains wha happens at the end of that physical battle:

"And the remnant were slain with the sword of him that sat upon th horse, which sword proceeded out of his mouth: and all the fowls wer filled with their flesh."

Chapter 6

The Final Countdown

Will the world end after the Battle of Armageddon described in Revelation? Many believe this will happen, but that's not what the Bible describes. Revelation explains that after the world recovers from Armageddon there will be a thousand years of peace; with Satan locked away in that 'bottomless pit.' That bottomless pit is a synonym for warfare. This means there will be no war during the millennium, that thousand years. The influence, the souls, of the first beast and the second beast, those two who created and strengthened Islam, will be burning in a fiery place during that time. (My conclusion is that Muhammad was the first beast, the antichrist; and Obama was the second beast, that false prophet who praised Muhammad's greatness.)

This means that Islam will be wiped from the face of the earth forever. This is clearly described in Revelation, Chapter 18. Islam is defined as Babylon the Great; that description coming from Chapter 17. Chapter 18 details the finality of Islam, beginning in verse 20:

"Rejoice over her, thou heaven, and ye holy apostles and prophets; for God hath avenged you on her. And a mighty angel took up a stone like a great millstone, and cast it into the sea, saying, Thus with violence shall that great city Babylon be thrown down, and shall be found no more at all." Verse 24 concludes, "And in her (Babylon - a religion is

53

referred to as a woman) was found the blood of prophets, and of saints
and of all that were slain upon the earth."

After the thousand years have expired (without Islam) there will b
another great war, again created by Satan. The world population wil
have increased greatly during that thousand years. That explanatio
begins in Chapter 20, verse 7:

"And when the thousand years are expired, Satan shall be loosed ou
of his prison (the absence of warfare) 8) And shall go out to deceiv
the nations which are in the four quarters of the earth, Gog and Magog
to gather them together to battle: the number of whom is as the san
of the sea. 9) And they went up on the breadth of the earth, an
compassed the camp of the saints about, and the beloved city: and fir
came down from God out of heaven and devoured them. 19) And th
devil that deceived them was cast into the lake of fire and brimstone
where the beast and the false prophet are, and shall be tormented da
and night for ever and ever."

Now, let's pause and consider the false claims of global warming an
the impending disaster it will cause. The verse above says the numbe
of people involved in that final great battle will be as the sand of th
sea. In more modern terms, the population of the earth will hav
greatly increased; which in all likelihood will be the major cause c
that war. This written Word totally contradicts the prophesy of thos
global warming prophets who claim global warming will caus
desolation and destruction of our planet. How can the population b
greatly increased if global warming will destroy the good life as w
know it on our planet?

The remainder of Chapter 20 then describes the 'book of life' and th
second resurrection. The first resurrection was for the souls of thos
who were beheaded and refused the mark of the beast (Islam,) wh

according to verse 4, "lived and reigned with Christ a thousand years." Gog and Magog are not described; perhaps that's to be determined by later generations who will live closer to that time period. For example, a thousand years ago no one could have guessed the rise and name of Islam which didn't arise until the seventh century. Then, Islam was described only as 'Babylon the Great' by Apostle John as he wrote the book of Revelation. He didn't know the word 'Islam.' We don't know the meaning of Gog and Magog until that time clue arrives. And, there's also a clue that life on earth will continue even after that greater war prophesied to happen a thousand years after the Battle of Armageddon.

The name Armageddon is contrived from the ancient city of Megiddo which is now a ruin site that overlooks the Jezreel Valley near Haifa. That area was the site of many historical battles in long ago history. Now let's move past that great battle to happen a thousand years after Armageddon. Will life on earth continue to exist afterwards? Many believe the world will end at that time. The verses suggest otherwise, that life and nations will continue. For that, let's move to Chapters 21 and 22.

Referring to the 'New Jerusalem,' Chapter 21, verse 24, reads, "And the nations of them which are saved shall walk in the light of it: and the kings of the earth do bring their glory and honour into it." Chapter 22 adds more. Beginning with the first verse is written, "And he shewed me a pure river of water of life, clear as crystal, proceeding out of the throne of God and of the Lamb. 2) In the midst of the street of it, and on either side of the river, was there the tree of life, which bare twelve manner of fruits, and yielded her fruit every month: and the leaves of the tree were for the healing of the nations." Again, this refers to nations. So what does this mean? The clue to this answer is found in Proverbs.

Proverbs 15:4 reads, "A wholesome tongue is a tree of life: bu
perverseness therein is a breach in the spirit." In other parts o
Revelation waters, sea, and rivers refer to the sea of humanity. Th
rivers refer to the flow of generations. Perhaps these verses mean tha
those who follow the Word of God, from a foundation of the twelv
apostles, will be rewarded with those fruits and blessings. The others
as the river flows, are guided by those leaves; those wholesom
tongues of guidance and examples by those favored by God. Thi
conclusion strongly suggests life will continue on this planet until Go
decides otherwise.

In Daniel, Chapter 12, verse 7, Daniel asks about the end of time. Go
gave Daniel an answer that he didn't understand, so Daniel aske
again in verse 8: "And I heard, but I understood not: then said I, O m
Lord, what shall be the end of these things?" Verse 9 gave the reply
"And he said, Go thy way, Daniel: for the words are closed up an
sealed till the time of the end."

Many verses in Revelation say to be ready. This refers to two types c
readiness. First, is to be ready for one's soul to find salvation wit
Christ in Heaven. To do this one must believe and accept the Word c
God through Christ. Second is to be ready for those hardships that ar
described as the time of tribulation on earth. The next section wi
offer suggestions for that preparation.

Chapter 7

Be Prepared

Our perils in America and the rest of the Western world from these actions by Babylon and her spawn; those harlots and terrorists; Islam, will be caused by globalization, world trade, economics, transportation and attacks on our power grid. Our transportation system to transport repair parts, food, and other survival items such as medicines and tonics will be crippled. Things we need from other parts of the world, because of world trade and globalization will not be available to us because enough ships will not be on the oceans, and cargo planes will not be in the air. The millions of trucks now clogging our major highways will be greatly reduced if not eliminated totally by damage or terrorism. Our survival will be as that of medieval or frontier days. Our nation is no longer prepared for that basic survival.

Christ cautioned many times in Revelation to be prepared; don't be caught naked, as in Chapter 16, verse 15:

"Behold, I come as a thief. Blessed is he that watcheth, and keepeth his garments, lest he walk naked, and they see his shame."

We must consider another possibility not to be 'caught naked.' That is to consider the possibility that North Korea, with all its bluster about building a nuclear arsenal to attack the United States, might be surreptitiously building that nuclear capability for Iran. A nuclear attack against the United States would mean total annihilation fo North Korea; certainly they must realize that. If that's the case, the what other purpose do they have for that nuclear threat; other than t assist Iran in its pledge to 'wipe Israel off the face of the earth?'

Of course, this is only one of the great cautions to be prepared. Th next verse in that reference describes the beginning of the Battle o Armageddon which will bring great horrors, especially in and aroun Israel. But, how must we prepare? We are warned of death b starvation, thirst, the sword, and beasts. Next are some ideas t consider for that preparation. We begin with considerations to protec ourselves from death by the 'sword.'

Protect Yourself - Own A Weapon

The most expedient preparation is to own a defensive weapon. If yo don't own one now, then this should be your first priority. It doesn matter if you agree with gun ownership or not - get a weapon, unles you desire to die 'by the sword' as indicated above. You must not b naked and without defense; especially if you have a family. If yo won't protect them in times of hardship; who will? If every qualifie person in America owns a weapon, and our enemies know it, then w likely would never have to fire those weapons. A hostile enemy wi not attack a target they know will kill them. We must let every Islami terrorist know they will die if they attack us. Even if they have suicid bombers, they will soon run out of volunteers. But, Islamic killers ar not the only great danger that might arise.

There's a serious consideration, however, before you buy that weapor That is to make sure you buy ammunition for it at the same time otherwise you might own a weapon that's useless. Recently, there wa a shortage of some ammunition during the Obama years, for obviou reasons, and that could happen again. It would be easier and simpler for a despotic leader to disarm people by eliminating the availability of ammunition. Millions of weapons have been handed down from generation to generation, and are therefore unaccountable. The government has no tracer information on these weapons. Most likely, any weapon purchased within the past few years is now recorded at the new NSA center in Bluffdale, Utah. Also, be aware that any new ammunition purchases, especially with a credit card or a check, will also be recorded at that site. Don't be surprised if sometime in the future certain items may be restricted from cash purchasing. Do it now!

Also, there's another danger that lurks closer to home. It's described as 'Wormwood.' Wormwood is a great star that fell from heaven when the third angel blew the trumpet, announcing horrible things would happen. This was not a star of course, but something that affected citizens of the earth. The word condition might have been used to describe it instead of a star falling. But the word 'great' gave the condition great significance. It's an unusual event included with the other great events in this chapter, including war and natural disasters. (Revelation 8:11)

In effect, this is a description of the great impact of drugs upon our society; so great in fact that it will become a danger during the time of tribulation. The word 'wormwood' describes a family of plants that grow in the wild. The plant is mostly a source of absinthe and opiates, but one variety produces a product that's considered artificial marijuana. In general, however, it describes the increased use of drugs; so much increase that it becomes a serious danger.

Just imagine what desperate and extreme measures users might do in their attempts to get more drugs. During this time of tribulation, would they invade your home, kill everyone, then plunder your belongings to

59

trade or sell for more drugs? Perhaps you might consider your disdain of owning a weapon. Perhaps you might no longer believe the arguments of those gun-haters. To comply with their ideas might get you and your family killed. Then it's too late to consider owning one

Prepare Not to Starve

According to Revelation, and mentioned in three places, hunger will be one of the greatest hardships during the tribulation period. Each person or each family must decide how to prepare for this horrible event. One way, and of course the most obvious way, is to prepare to grow your own food during this period. This is a simple answer for farmers who have acreage and are trained in the techniques of farming

Most farmers with large gardens also know how to can their produce for the more austere times. However, those who have no acreage or space enough to grow a garden must have other alternatives. It's uncertain if farmers can produce enough to provide for the massive hunger that will occur. Probably not; and shipping and transportation will be greatly reduced if not totally eliminated to move produce long distances. So, other options must be explored before the need arises. You must be prepared.

One option growing in popularity is to accumulate large stocks of those meals with a long life span, some up to twenty or twenty-five years. Presently, there are two major advertisers of these products, but likely there are more. For some, this is not the best option and for two reasons. First is the cost. They are more expensive than comparable meals. Second is that they require water to prepare the meal. 'Just add water and heat' the ads say. But what if you don't have water or heat

Another reasonable alternative is to buy canned food; and it's certainly the least expensive for those on a limited budget. One might ask 'why not stock frozen food?' The answer is simple; likely there will be little or no electricity during the worst times of the tribulation. Canned food offers another great advantage. All canned foods include water and liquids in the cans. This could be one source of liquid to prevent severe thirst. Hunger and thirst are two of the four horrors described to happen during the tribulation period. But, one might be concerned about the cost, and loss through 'best by' dates on the cans.

To counter the cost of canned food one must remember the main objective during the tribulation period is survival. Therefore, quality food and the 'food you like' are not that important. The most important thing to consider is cost per unit (ounce) and 'best by' dates. For examples: most food stores and supermarkets have rotating special prices on their canned vegetables. Some cans normally priced above a dollar are put on special prices such as half that to draw customers to the store. That's the time to buy that product in quantity; as many as the store will allow. And, there's another option that might even be better; the dollar discount store.

Almost all canned food products at the 'dollar stores' are priced at a dollar. However, many of those canned items contain more than twice as much as those priced less at regular supermarkets. It's not unusual to find three times the volume at the same or lower price. In either case the 'best by' date must be considered. Since this year is 2018, the beginning stock of food should begin with dates of 2019 and beyond. Some 'best by' dates now reach as far as 2022. How much should you buy and preposition? That depends on the size of your family and those you intend to support during those trying times. It also depends on your space availability for storage. Once stored, however, those dates become important. To manage the dates, keep them stocked separately by year.

Rotation is the answer. Once you have the sufficient stock on hand

then future purchases become normal purchases for the current time
And for those items nearing the 'best by' dates that haven't been use
there's another good answer. Simply donate them to local 'foo
pantries' and other charities that offer food to the needy. But, don'
consider it a loss; instead consider it another tool of God's influenc
upon humans helping humans. And in some cases it might even be th
source of a tax deduction.

Two other alternatives regarding a food source might also b
considered. First, don't forget to have a large supply of fish hook
fishing line, and other auxiliary fishing equipment. Fish an
crustaceans are usually available in most bodies of water. Eve
crayfish exist is small streams. Second, powerful air rifles are now o
the market for shooting small game; and some have silencers, whic
is an advantage if you are trying to remain safely and quietly in th
background.

Have a Water Source

According to the Words, during tribulation many will die from: th
sword, hunger, thirst, and beasts, so one must also plan for a wate
source. For the many who live near a water source such as river
lakes, and natural springs that will not be a great problem; excep
possibly for the purity of the water. This problem may be countered b
using a water purification system (personal ones are available fc
about twenty dollars; often called a straw) or by boiling the water c
using an evaporation apparatus. There are also other methods c
purification including the use of certain tablets. Regarding 'boilin
water' perhaps this is the best place to discuss fire and heat.

Okay, I realize I should avoid references in this conclusion, but there'
one that's too important to ignore. It's Revelation 7:4 which cautior
against hurting the 'trees.' Trees are also mentioned in Chapter 5

which might suggest we not destroy too many of our trees during this time of tribulation; when we are likely to be without sources of fire and heat. Can you imagine how many trees would be destroyed as a source of heat for billions of people on the earth trying to stay warm for three to seven years? Trees once were the major source of heat, but the earth had many less inhabitants. Even so, at that time many of our forests were devastated. But today there's an alternative - solar cookers and ovens.

There are several types of solar ovens, some simple and some more complex. At the present time they are somewhat expensive; the better ones in the three-hundred dollar range. However, considering their utility during difficult times that extra cost might be well worth the expense, especially if you are not in an area where wood is available; dry wood. Once a tree is cut it has to dry before it can be used for fuel. I know, because in my youth my family and many families used wood for the stove and the fireplace. We didn't have electricity until I was twelve years old.

Those solar cookers will work when there is even medium sunshine, so using them wouldn't be hassle free, but it's certainly a reasonable alternative when the sun is shining. Most, at this time, are not mass produced which means if there's a sudden demand for them they might not be available. And, there are also optional solar tubes for heating water. These are less expensive and can also be used for cooking like a stove, with the addition of an insert tray. But, what about those times when the sun isn't adequate to make those solar cookers effective? The other alternative, of course, is firewood; which likely will be the primary source for most survivors. This brings a question of how to start that fire without a match.

A large stock of matches or cigarette lighters or other fuel lighters might be the most obvious answer of how to start a fire. And, there are

two alternative ways, just in case matches don't work and fuel i
exhausted.

The first alternative is the camp-style striker method. There are severa
interpretations of the striker, where a rod is scraped against a starte
producing sparks to start a fire tender. There's another alternative
however, that most people never consider. And, when the sun i
shining it's definitely the most effective - the common magnifyin,
glass. Using the sun, a magnifying glass focused to a fine point o:
paper or other tender will start a fire.

A very strong magnifying glass is always more effective, but a weake
magnifier will work well during the hottest times of day. The bes
news about the magnifying glass is that water doesn't hurt it, and th
fuel never runs out. I have four strong ones pre-positioned fo
emergencies. Once prepared for these three threats, there's still one t
consider. It's introduced as beasts, which most certainly would mea
organisms, diseases, and pestilence.

Prepare for Health Disasters

If this tribulation time is as horrendous as written in the Bible, the
many people will die from communicable diseases and maladies tha
are somewhat controllable today. Today, we have medicines an
immunizations to prevent and combat things such as flu an
pneumonia. Just imagine what would happen if these protections wer
not available for three to seven years. In large groups, these horro
would spread like wildfire, and only the healthiest and hardiest wou
survive, especially if complicated without heat to ease the freezing an
wet nights. Without proper medications the only defense would be t
wear masks and avoid large groups during these periods of epidemic
But, these maladies are not the only threats to survival.

Two other serious threats will be ticks and mosquitoes. These have been serious problems throughout history. In our modern day, and in our modern societies, repellants ordinarily repel these malicious enemies; but will repellants be available during the tribulation period? Not likely. One possibility is to try to anticipate the beginning time and have as much on hand as possible. If you have too much, your friends and family might need help. And, if you spend any time at all outdoors, especially in warmer times, always check every inch of your skin for ticks. They are very small until they gorge themselves with your blood; then it might be too late. If your home is not perfectly sealed, don't forget to sleep under netting at night.

Another common problem often arises when in survival mode; especially outdoors. That's the problem of infection from scratches and other wounds. Briars, thorns, and broken sharp sticks abound everywhere in the outdoors, even in the safety of your enclosed yard. If an infection occurs from one of these pricks, scratches, or cuts there likely will not be medical aid nearby to help you. Of course, the logical answer to defend yourself against these 'beasts' is to have an adequate stock of antiseptics and antibiotics on hand to last the duration. These beasts will kill people as surely as guns, hunger, and thirst; and often with long-lasting pain. Be Prepared.

65

Chapter 8

Finally

My daily research for over seven years strongly convinces me that Barack Hussein Obama is that second beast identified in Revelation, Chapter 13, as the False Prophet. That False Prophet claims to be a Christian, but he speaks and praises only Muhammad and Islam. "And he exerciseth all the power of the first beast (Muhammad - a national leader,) and causeth the earth and them which dwell therein to worship the first beast, whose deadly wound was healed."

During Obama's administration he took no direct military action to implement the policies of that first beast, but his words and actions caused many Islamic principles to grow and be acknowledged in the United States and throughout the world. His actions (inactions) caused that image to the beast, that caliphate in the Middle East, to be built.

And, although he is no longer President of the United States, his charge from Satan will not be lessened. He will take no direct actions against any nation, but his persuasive and deceptive blasphemy will cause others to be the hands of Satan to fulfill Satan's oath to remove God from heaven. Obama's deceptions and lying wonders will continue to cause a divided and confused nation; a nation in which within that confusion many will not recognize God's promise of everlasting salvation.

Barack Obama will not go quietly and remain in the background as loyal supporter of the United States of America: One nation unde God. As Chapter 13 reveals; he will cause things of Satan to happer Through his efforts, words, and deeds, many of his followers wi willingly accept that 'mark of the beast' to be placed on thei foreheads.

Although he is no longer a formal part of our governmer administration, he will continue to use words and actions outside th government to create strong divisions within our government. T fulfill Satan's plan he must continue to create division within ou nation so as not to allow our nation to come together as a nation unite under God.

And so here we are today; the world still under attack by Satan and hi evil Islamic beast. It's a beast so evil it kills everyone in its path; eve its own relatives and kinsmen. It's an evil so great not even total powe would satisfy itself. There are no limits to the breadth or time of i horror; but its primary and sworn aim is to destroy God in heavei This explains why God will turn his wrath against this horrible beas that has challenged Him. Islam has spread to the seven heads (thos seven continents) and threatens to unleash even more horror agains those who worship God.

Within the Words, God has acknowledged that challenging swor threat from Satan. When the time prophesied arrives He will totall destroy that evil; for at least a thousand years when Satan will escap from that dark pit (the conscience of men) to spread evil once agaii The question of our time, however, is what will happen to ou generation when our Apocalypse begins. Will our world still exist ¿ it is? Chapters 21 and 22 of Revelation answer this question:

Chapter 21, Verse 24 reads, "And the nations of them which are save

68

shall walk in the light of it: (referring to the new city of Jerusalem) and the kings of the earth do bring their glory and honour into it."

Chapter 22, Verse 2, "In the midst of the street of it, and on either side of the river, was there the tree of life, which bare twelve manner of fruits, and yielded her fruit every month: and the leaves of the tree were for the healing of the nations." Verse 4 adds, "And they that see his face; and his name shall be in their foreheads." Verse 12 warns, "And, behold, I come quickly; and my reward is with me, to give every man according to his work shall be."

According to the Words, the physical world will continue to exist even after the great tribulation; there is hope for humanity. In the end, according to the last verses in the Bible, it will be a better world without the presence of that strange god to wreak evil upon the earth.

The Catholic Church

Before I close I must write a word about the Catholic Church; so often accused of being that woman Babylon, or the site of the Antichrist. Nothing could be further from the truth. Had it not been for the Catholic Church established by Constantine the Great, Christianity might not have survived those vicious attacks by Romans, other despots, and Muslims.

From a vision during the night before the Battle at Milvian Bridge in October, 312 A.D., Constantine had a revelation to fight that battle under a Christian symbol. The next day before the battle he had his men paint a Christian cross on their shields. After winning that battle against Maxentius the divided Rome was then reunited under Constantine the 'Great.' He later formed the Roman Catholic Church. That was approximately 325 A.D. Then Rome protected Christianity another 350 years. That event is recorded in Revelation, Chapter 12, verse 14:

"And to the woman (Christianity) were given two wings of a grea
eagle, that she might fly into the wilderness, into her place, where sh
is nourished for a time, and times, and half a time, from the face of th
serpent."

Codes were given in verse six to reveal this time, and times, and ha
a time is approximately 350 years. Considering that an eagle was th
symbol of Rome, and Constantine was considered 'Great' these code
mean that Rome protected Christianity until approximately the mi
seventh century; when Christianity was again attacked by Muhamma
and his Islamists. Eventually Islam gained complete control over thos
Asian nations that had been the home of many Christian
Notwithstanding, the Catholic Church still remained the protector c
Christianity.

The Catholic Church remained a stalwart protector and source c
Christian principles and leadership. Furthermore, the Catholic Churc
has never been and will never become that Mystery Babylon, or th
home of the Antichrist; for it has never been 'drunken with the bloo
of the saints and with the blood of the martyrs of Jesus.' Furthermor
the Catholic Church has never disavowed the belief that Jesus Chri
is the Son of God. Although many, including myself, do not agree wit
many of their activities and principles; since they accept the bas
foundation and worship Jesus Christ as the Son of God, I'm sure the
will be welcomed into God's salvation when their time is called.

I must add a final comment regarding this information, thes
interpretations and these observations. These are made from my seve
years of almost daily reading of Revelation and associated Books i
the Bible. They are not made from visions or any special words give
to me. These are merely my personal interpretations of what I hav

read and analyzed.

God bless America, and protect Israel.

About the Author

Will Clark's author experiences began by writing inspection and evaluation reports in the U.S. Air Force. He is a retired Air Force officer and a Vietnam veteran, serving in Saigon from 1966 to 1967. His other overseas assignments include Misawa, Japan and Ankara, Turkey; where he visited the ancient sites of the Seven Churches.

In 1995, as a 'Friends of Education' study skills project, he authored a book, How to Learn, to encourage students to improve their grades in DeSoto County, Mississippi. Education supporters printed and distributed four thousand copies. The following school year he wrote a weekly education column for a local newspaper, The DeSoto County Tribune. He also taught an adult GED class. His book, How to Learn, has been updated and is now available everywhere.

His next published book was School Bells and Broken Tales, a parody of nursery rhyme characters, also a motivation and education book for children. Other books include Shades of Retribution, a historical novel, and Simply Success, a motivation guide for students and employees.

His action novel, The Atlantis Crystal, is the first of a trilogy based on Atlantis and crystals. The other two books are: She Waits in Atlantis, and Return to Atlantis. This trilogy is based on his travels while assigned to Turkey, site of the ancient city of Troy. His latest political thriller is: America 20XX: The New World Order.

The past five years he has devoted his full time to the study, research, and writing of an analysis of the Book of Revelation and the danger of Satan, that beast that guides Islam.

Things We Must Never Forget

Benghazi

Why were four Americans killed?
Where was Hillary Clinton while it was happening?
Where was Barack Obama while it was happening?
Why did they lie and blame the event on a video?
Why were rescuers on 'stand by' told to 'stand down?'

Fast and Furious

Who authorized the operation?
Why did the operation continue after weapons were lost?
Why did the procedure have no procedure?
Why weren't tracking devices used?

The IRS Scandal

What was the highest level involved?
Who initiated it?
Why hasn't anyone been fired or reprimanded?
What dangers could be unleashed by this organization?

Greatest Quotes
of Our Time

Michelle Obama
February 18, 2008
"For the first time in my adult life I am proud of my country."
(Age 44)

Barack Obama
March 9, 2008"We are no longer a Christian nation - at least not just."
September 25, 2012
Remarks to the UN General Assembly
"The future must not belong to those who slander Islam."

Nancy Pelosi
March 9, 2010
"We have to pass the bill so that you can find out what is in it."

Hillary Clinton
January 23, 2013
"What difference, at this point, does it make?"

December 3, 2014
"...showing respect even for one's enemies, trying to understand and insofar as psychologically possible, empathize with their perspective and point of view."

Other Books by the Author

Novels:

Shades of Retribution
The Atlantis Crystal
She Waits in Atlantis
Return to Atlantis
America 20XX: The New World Order
666: Mark of the Beast
Death Drones: 2025

Children's Books:

Forest Trails and Fairy Tales
Wishing Wells and Broken Tales
Student Study Skills
American Heroes: Students Who Learn

Non-Fiction:

Simply Success
The Education Jungle
How to Learn
The Day America Died
Obama's Ring: The Seat of Satan
Managing Without Conflict
The Peer Pressure Monster
Denied 3 Times
The War on Christians
Who is the Antichrist

Islamic Two-Headed Beast
Islam Attacks the Whore
The Second Beast
Secrets of the Seven Churches
Two Woman of the Apocalypse
Islam's Bloodthirsty Sword
Once Upon A Revelation: About Islam
America Gasps
God's Islamaknowbe Warriors
A Reason to Believe
Islam's Three Beasts
Donald Trump Destroys Babylon the Great
He Defeats Hillary, Obama, and the Antichrist

Made in the USA
Columbia, SC
28 May 2018